Cool! Whoa! Ah and Oh!

What Is an Interjection?

To the Hernan grandkids
—B.P.C.

Cool! Whoa! Ah and Oh!

What Is an Interjection?

by Brian P. Cleary

illustrations by Brian Gable

M MILLBROOK PRESS / MINNEAPOLIS

An interjection is a word

or phrase that helps show feeling,

4

as in, "oh, my!" or "Help!" or "Yikes— a spider's on my ceiling!"

Interjections can be found in different parts of speech.

You'll see one in a pronoun here:
"Dear me! That's one good peach!"

From time to time, they're adjectives, like, "Good! There's pepperoni!"

They also may be adverbs, like,

PEPPERONI

"Indeed! The cook was Tony!"

Sometimes they show up as nouns, as in this case: "The jerk!

The fool!
He used my skates and bike.

Now neither of them work!"

These words are little signs to show
When meaning should be stressed.

Like, "oh my gosh! I didn't know today we've got a test!"

15

Our sentences can have more thrills,

be action-packed or gory

When words like Zap!

and Pow!

and Pop!

are added to our story.

In getting folks' attention,
they can also come in handy,

as in, "Hey, you! Look over here!
This tree is growing candy!"

Sometimes interjections
can be used to show your grief,

as in, "We shared a locker,
but alas, he was a thief."

They're useful when you want to show

amazement, awe, or shock,

like when a pirate hollers,
"ARG!

My dinghy dinged the dock."

"Oh!" can show surprise or pain and works as well with pleading.

Like, "oh! oh! oh! Please call on me.

I'd love to do this reading."

"Ah!" might go before

"That's good."

Or "Now I comprehend."

Or even, "Well, we thought we'd try."

Or "I can't find my friend!"

27

Cool! Amazing! WoW!

can also go in this collection,

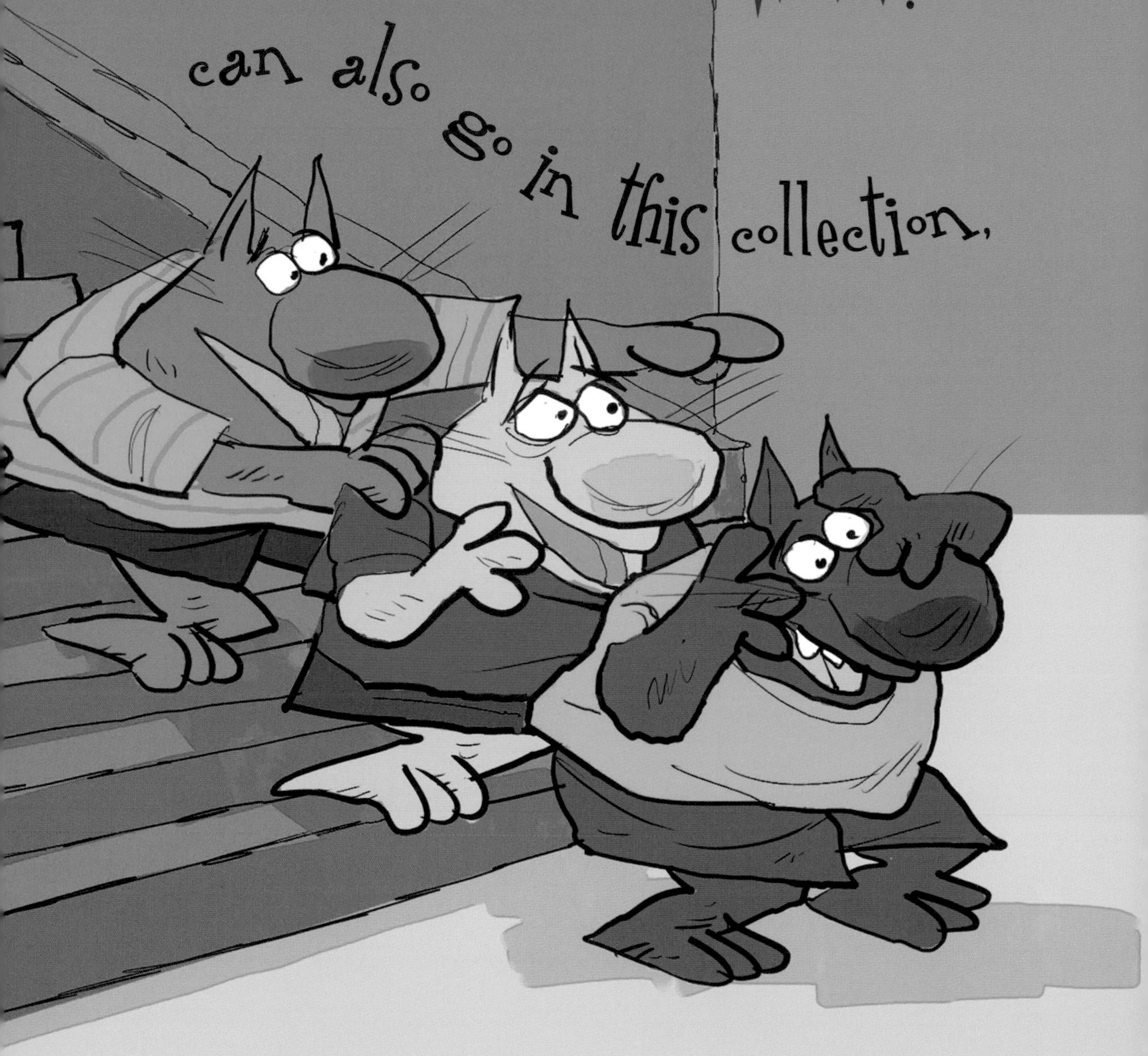

'cause now you know the answer to

"What is an interjection?"

So what is an **interjection?**
Do you know?

Find activities, games, and more at
www.brianpcleary.com

ABOUT THE AUTHOR & ILLUSTRATOR

BRIAN P. CLEARY is the author of the best-selling Words Are CATegorical® series as well as the Math Is CATegorical®, Food Is CATegorical™, Adventures in Memory™, and Sounds Like Reading® series. He has also written Six Sheep Sip Thick Shakes: And Other Tricky Tongue Twisters, The Punctuation Station, and several other books. Mr. Cleary lives in Cleveland, Ohio.

BRIAN GABLE is the illustrator of many Words Are CATegorical® books and the Math Is CATegorical® series. Mr. Gable also works as a political cartoonist for the Globe and Mail newspaper in Toronto, Canada.

Text copyright © 2011 by Brian P. Cleary
Illustrations copyright © 2011 by Lerner Publishing Group, Inc.

Millbrook Press
A division of Lerner Publishing Group, Inc.
241 First Avenue North
Minneapolis, MN 55401 U.S.A.

Website address: www.lernerbooks.com

Library of Congress Cataloging-in-Publication Data

Cleary, Brian P., 1959-
   Cool! whoa! ah and oh! : what is an interjection? / by Brian P. Cleary ; illustrated by Brian Gable.
   p.   cm. — (Words are CATegorical)
   ISBN: 978-1-58013-594-8 (lib. bdg. : alk. paper)
   1. English language—Interjections. I. Gable, Brian, 1949- II. Title.
 PE1355.C54 2011
   428.2—dc22   2010026263

Manufactured in the United States of America
1 — DP — 12/15/10